D1639474

THANK YOU, GOD

THANK YOU, GOD

A Book of Children's Prayers

Compiled by
Lisa Potts

with drawings by Lesley Harker

Hodder & Stoughton
LONDON   SYDNEY   AUCKLAND

British Library Cataloguing in Publication Data:
A record for this book is available from the British Library.

ISBN 0 340 70981 2

Typeset in Monotype Plantin Schoolbook by
Strathmore Publishing Services, London N7

Printed and bound in Great Britain by
Mackays of Chatham PLC, Chatham, Kent

Hodder and Stoughton Ltd
A division of Hodder Headline PLC
338 Euston Road, London NW1 3BH

*This book is dedicated
to all the children in the nursery
and the staff and parents,
including my own dear parents,
who suffered so much on 8 July 1996.*

Contents

Acknowledgements

I would like to thank all the children who worked so hard on the prayers included in the book, and Hodder and Stoughton for publishing it.

I want to thank the parents and guardians of the children whose prayers are printed here, for their permission to publish this work.

I would also like thank the following people for all their love, help and support throughout the past year:

Lee Potts, Helen Fullard, Nici Wilkins, Nici Nail, Clare Hughes, Marc Street, Paul Kilvington, Dawn Evans, Pam Teece, Peter Smith, Martin McGlown, all staff and parents at St Luke's School, St Joseph's Church and 1st Merry Hill leaders and Brownies.

Also thanks to the rest of my family and friends who I love dearly but am unable to mention personally.

Introduction

On 8 July 1996 a terrible incident took place at St Luke's Infant and Nursery School involving me, my nursery class and another teacher, Miss Hawes. It was a beautiful day and we were having a teddy bears' picnic with the children and some of the parents who had come to help us. Suddenly, out of nowhere, a strange-looking man came running towards us carrying something. At first I couldn't make out what was happening or what he was waving around; then I saw that it was a machete. My first reaction was that it was a toy knife but when he actually started to attack one of the parents the terrible reality struck me. He jumped over the fence and started to attack me and some of the children who were trying frantically to run away. It was such an unreal experience; like a nightmare from which I kept thinking I would wake up.

After that terrifying experience we all managed to get away alive but sadly some of the children were badly hurt with facial and head injuries. I was left with very serious injuries but I managed somehow to shield the children from the worst of the attack and to get myself and them out of the nursery.

That day was the most horrendous of my life and no one at the school will ever forget it. I thank God that no one died on that day, even though so much pain has been suffered, both mental and physical. The scars can never disappear but I hope that with God's help we will slowly come to terms with such an awful experience and learn to live with it.

The story hit the nation very quickly and came soon after the horrors of Dunblane. It seemed shocking that anything similar could happen again. I was sent over three thousand cards and letters from all over the country and even from overseas. Some of the letters were so comforting. I realised that there were many, many good people but this at first was hard to believe and accept after an experience which had torn apart my faith in humanity.

I had six months off school because of my injuries, as I was unable to perform many of those tasks which we take for granted each day. Those six months were easier than I had expected, probably because I had set myself the goal to return to St Luke's and face all the fears and flashbacks of that day. I returned to St Luke's in January 1997 with great feelings of apprehension but the welcome from the children took all of these fears away. It was marvellous to see those children whom I had seen so brutally attacked, playing so happily and innocently, and I felt great wonder at their hope and trust. But I knew also that scars had been left and I hope that with time their memories will fade. At the moment I feel as an adult that there is nothing of that day that I will ever forget but I know that one day the sun will start to shine through me like it used to.

As a child I went to Sunday school from the age of three. There I spent a lot of time talking to God and drawing pictures and listening to stories. As I got older I enjoyed writing my own prayers about the world and all the varied experiences around me. So when I was asked to compile this prayer book I hoped that the children I have contact with would enjoy writing prayers as much as I had done.

The prayer book consists of twenty headings relating to children's experiences at different times in their lives. Most of the prayers have been written by children, a few by me. I had many wonderful prayers to choose from and I thank all the children who participated and supported the project.

The children come from St Luke's School, from my local church where I run a crèche on Sundays, and also from the Brownie pack where I am an assistant Brownie leader called 'Sunny Owl'.

The ages of the children range from four to

twelve years. You can see how the experience of God changes as children get older. For example, the lovely section on heaven illustrates this.

Prayer is a great natural response to life, especially with children as children respond to life so innocently and spontaneously. Often one short prayer will express many different parts of their day.

One of the prayers which touched my heart was that of Francesca Quintyne, aged four. Francesca was one of the children who was attacked on that dreadful day. She has included so many different aspects of her life in one big expression of thanks. Every time I read this prayer it brings a tear to my eyes and a smile to my face:

Dear Jesus
　I love school
　I love mummy and nanny
　I love Miss Potts and Miss Poole
　I love my friends
　I was poorly in hospital with Miss Potts but I am better now.

Amen

The first prayer in this book is the school prayer of St Luke's which the children pray every morning. It is simple for children to read and understand.

I do hope that this book will be enjoyed by all

Introduction

age ranges and that parents and teachers will find it helpful. I trust that it will give encouragement to search all areas of our lives and share them with God. I have shared both happy and sad times with God and he has brought great joy to my life, as well as great sorrow, but in the end I know that he listens to all our prayers.

Thank you to 'my' children, and may this book be one way of saying 'thank you' to the God who takes care of us even in the darkest times.

Lisa Potts
1997

St Luke's School prayer

Bless our school
that by working together
and playing together
we may learn
to love one another.

Amen

1

Christmas

Dear Lord

Christmas is a very special time of year. It's full of laughter, presents, food, playing, and people full of the Christmas spirit. Please let us not forget the real meaning of Christmas, that your son Jesus was born in a stable in Bethlehem many years ago.

Amen

Lisa Potts

Dear God

Thank you very much for baby Jesus. He is very special.

Amen

Linford Davis, aged 4

Dear Lord

Thank you for the day Jesus was born. We call this day Christmas. This is a day when we celebrate the good news and hope that we can all live in peace and harmony together.

Amen

Katy Tilt, aged 9

Dear God

I love Christmas, it is such a happy time. Thank you for all the lovely presents that we give and receive at Christmas time. Let us not forget that Jesus was born.

Amen

Sophie Corbett, aged 8

Dear Lord

Every day is a special day but the most special day in the year is the day that Jesus was born in that dirty stable with no clean blankets. Help us to remember at Christmas time the people who have no food or warmth. Let us remember how lucky we are.

Amen

Laura Littleton, aged 8

Dear God

Thank you for all the presents and cards we get at Christmas. They are all really nice.

Amen

Reena Chopra, aged 4

Dear Lord

Thank you for all the beautiful presents that are given to us by people who love us. Let us try not to forget those people who don't get presents. Help us not to be selfish or greedy this Christmas time.

Amen

Lisa Potts

2

Easter

Dear Lord

Thank you for Easter because Jesus was killed on the cross and he rose from the dead. Thank you for Easter eggs and your son Jesus.

Amen

Rachel Emery, aged 7

Dear Lord

You loved us so much that you died for us all on a cross. This day is called Good Friday. It makes us all so sad that you died for us but on Easter day you arose. You are alive again and listening to our prayers always.

Amen

Lisa Potts

Dear Lord

Thank you for Easter. Thank you for the eggs we have. Help us not to be greedy and make ourselves ill as we must remember that there will be children who won't have any eggs at all.

Amen

Lucy Arnold, aged 8

Dear Lord

I like chocolate eggs. They taste so nice. You made every egg in the whole wide world. You are a really nice man.

Amen

Nakita Banger, aged 4

Dear Lord

Thank you for Easter. Please help us to remember that Easter wouldn't be here without Jesus. Help us to remember the true meaning of Easter, Jesus died for everyone. As we eat Easter eggs at Easter remember the time that Jesus was tempted in the wilderness to turn away from God and do wrong things but you didn't and that's what makes you so special.

Amen

Danielle Cook, aged 9

Easter

Dear Jesus

Easter time is full of pretty flowers and animals. You made them all.

Amen

Rajanpreet Dhaliwall, aged 5

Dear Lord

You suffered so much hurt and pain for us all. You died on the cross to take away our sins. This shows that you loved us all so much. Let us never forget this.

Amen

Lisa Potts

3

Harvest

Dear Lord

Thank you for the crops that grow,
corn, oat and wheat.
In the field and in the wind
all growing for us to eat,
growing, growing all the time,
like an act or silent mime,
made into bread and cereal too.
Shining in the sun like new.

Amen

Amy Vaughan, aged 7

Dear Lord

Thank you for Harvest time, for all the ripe fruit and vegetables, for all the beautiful colours we see at this time of year. Help us not to take all of this for granted.

Amen

Lisa Potts

Dear Lord

Thank you for the crops and hay for the horses to lie on and eat, thank you for the farmers and their tractors because they do so much for us. Thank you that we are able to have a Harvest festival and then we give all the food out to people who haven't got much food. Let us remember these people at this time of year.

Amen

Clare Portik, aged 8

Dear Lord

Thank you for all the food that is given at Harvest time. Let us think about the people in the land who don't have very much food at all.

Amen

Emma Sanderson, aged 6

Dear God

Harvest is a time when we give food and put it all together and then we give it out to people who don't have much food. Let us try not just to give at Harvest but all the time through the year.

Amen

Emily Hills, aged 8

Dear God

Thank you for the Harvest time. Thank you for the farmers who grow all the fruit like strawberries, apples, plums and pears. Thank you for the vegetables like carrots, peas, cabbages and cauliflowers. They are really nice to eat.

Amen

Zoe Campbell, aged 7

Dear Lord

At this time of year we must try and remember the farmers who work so hard in preparing all the wheat, barley and oats for it to be made into so many different types of food for us all to eat. We thank you for all the food that is gathered in and stored for the winter days.

Amen

Lisa Potts

4

Birthdays

Dear Father God

We thank you so much each year for our birthday. It is such a special and exciting time. As we get older, help us to grow and learn to be more like you every day.

Amen

Lisa Potts

Dear God

Thank you for birthdays special and
loving,
Thank you for people kind and caring.
On birthdays we have lots of friends
it feels like birthdays never end.
Thank you, Lord, for birthdays.

Amen

Clare Russel, aged 8

Birthdays

Dear Jesus

I like birthdays, I like presents and ballons. It is a nice day on everybody's birthday. Thank you God.

> Amen

Sarah Cadman, aged 5

Dear Lord

Presents, games and fun,
my birthday has just begun,
exciting laughter and joy,
I wonder what's inside my present – I
                    hope it's a toy.
Thank you Lord for such a special day,
I enjoyed it so much I have to say.

> Amen

Matthew Harper, aged 7

Dear Father God

Thank you for birthdays, for fun and jokes. I like cakes and presents. I like to dress in my fancy clothes on my birthday and I like it when all my friends come to my house. It makes me sad to think that some children don't have birthdays. I wish that I could have everybody who doesn't have a birthday come to my house. Thank you God for birthdays, and, God, I love you.

Amen

Autumn Anderson, aged 7

Dear Lord

Today is a special day. It's my birthday. Thank you for all the wonderful gifts that are given to me. Let us remember that today someone else somewhere in the world is celebrating their birthday but they might not be as lucky as I am. So help me to be grateful.

Amen

Lisa Potts

Dear God

Thank you for birthdays. They are so special, and thank you that my friends can come to my house for a party where we can play games and have fun together and eat lots of party food like crisps and cakes and jelly and ice cream. I love birthdays.

Amen

Rachel Smith, aged 7

5

Bonfire night

Dear Lord

Thank you for bonfire night, with the blazing bonfires, the rainbow-coloured fireworks and the jumping sparklers. Please help us to be aware of the blazing fire and not to play to near it.

Thank you for fire fighters and paramedics because it's always a busy month for them. Thank you that you gave them these wonderful skills to help us.

Amen

Hannah Swatman, aged 10

Dear God

Thank you for bonfire night. It is such a fun time. We can see all of the sparklers and fireworks, but we have to be careful of the fires because little children might run into the fires. Please take care of us all on bonfire night.

Amen

Letisha Quintyne, aged 7

Dear God

Thank you for the bonfires and sparklers and the fireworks in the sky. Let us be careful on this night as we could get badly hurt.

In Jesus's name Amen

Steffan Jackson, aged 7

Dear Lord

Thank you for bonfire night, for bonfires with such beautiful colours, for sparklers and fireworks whizzing and soaring so high up in the sky.

There is always such a lovely smell on bonfire night of hot food. Let us be very grateful for this special time.

       Amen

Lisa Potts

Dear Lord

Bonfire night is a very exciting time of year and it only comes but once a year. Help us to be careful and really enjoy ourselves. Let us look out for small children who don't understand the dangers of red-hot fires. Let us go out and wrap up warm in our hats, scarves and gloves as it is very cold.

Lord, help us to have fun and know that you are always with us.

Amen

Lisa Potts

Dear Lord

Thank you for colourful bonfires
that glisten in the night,
different shades of colours bright,
crackling fireworks,
snapping bonfires all the night.
We thank you Lord for all this.

Amen

Matthew Harris, aged 11

Dear God

Thank you Lord for bonfire night, for all the lovely noises there are, for the distant glow and the cheerful way the fires burn at night when it's cold and dark and miserable, so thank you Lord for bonfire night.

Amen

Michael Hills, aged 10

6

Holidays

Dear Lord

Holidays are so special. It doesn't matter whether we stay at home or if we go far away to another country, we know that you are always with us wherever we go or whatever we do.

Amen

Lisa Potts

Dear Father God

Let us be thankful to our parents who work hard to take us on holiday. Thank you God for the special time that we spend with our families and that you are always there keeping us safe from nasty things in the world.

Amen

Emma Christina Campbell, aged 8

Lord Jesus

Thank you for holidays when we go away to the seaside and we can pack our clothes into the suitcase and put it into the car. Thank you Jesus for keeping us safe when we travel in the car on the busy roads.

Amen

Ashley Evans, aged 7

Dear Lord

Thank you for holidays. They really cheer me up. I love to splash in the sea, to make sand castles on the beach and to collect shells to make decorations. Thank you Lord for holidays.

Amen

Jenny Smith, aged 8

Dear God

Thank you for sunny days when we can go on picnics with our friends. I love it when the sun shines brightly so that we can play on our bikes and have lots of fun. Thank you for holiday times.

Amen

Richard Tilt, aged 7

Dear God

Thank you that we have holidays so that we can have a rest and have lots of fun together. It is so good that we can sometimes go on holiday to the seaside where we can play in the sea and build sand castles.

Amen

Zena Patel, aged 7

Dear Lord

Let us be thankful that we can go on holidays with our families. Thank you, Lord, for giving people skills to make aeroplanes that can take us to other countries so we can see how other people live and work. You are a very special person.

Amen

Lisa Potts

7

Graces

Dear Lord

Bless this food, Lord, that we are about
to eat.

Thank you, Lord, that the table is so
neat.

Let us remember that for some children
this would only be a yearly treat.

Amen

Lisa Potts

Dear God

Thank you for this lovely food on this table. Let us not forget people who have no food at all.

Amen

Rachel Harris, aged 7

Dear Lord

Thank you for all the food like cake and chocolate and crisps and chips. They all are really nice.

Amen

Shanice Warner, aged 4

Dear God

Thank you for the food we eat. Thank you for the drinks we drink. Thank you for our mums and dads who cook our meals all day long. Thank you for the farmers who grow our food in the fields. Thank you for the bakers who bake our bread. Thank you for the cows who produce our milk. Thank you for the pigs who produce our pork, and last of all God thank you for me, to eat your food and drink your drink.

Amen

Michael Carter, aged 10

Dear Lord

Thank you for our food, breakfast dinner and tea. Please help those who are not as fortunate as us. They don't get nice big meals but they have to make do with what they've got. Please help us not to take things for granted and think of others.

Amen

Hannah Swatman, aged 10

Dear Lord

Thank you for all the food that we eat. It all tastes nice. I like crisps a real lot.

Amen

Terence White, aged 4

Dear Lord

Let us be thankful for this wonderful food we are about to eat. Let it give us strength so that we can do your work.

Amen

Lisa Potts

8

Heaven

Dear Lord

Heaven is a place where people go when they are old, but it is sad when young children go. Everybody who is good goes to heaven.

Amen

Alistair Smith, aged 5

Dear Lord

Heaven is a nice place to go to. There are lots of people there always smiling and they are never ever horrible. Only very good people go to heaven. Lord, I'm going to be good so I can go to heaven one day.

Amen

Darren Jones, aged 6

Dear God

I think heaven is good and good people go to heaven when they die. I think Jesus and you are in heaven. There are pretty flowers in heaven and everybody sings in heaven. It is sad when people die but I think that they will have a nice time in heaven.

Amen

Davina Patel, aged 7

Dear Lord

Heaven is a very happy place. We know this because no one has ever come down to say that they didn't like it. It is very sad when people die and leave us but very happy for them to spend time with you.

Amen

Emily Brettel, aged 8

Dear Lord

I thank you that we can have visions of heaven because of the stories you told and put in a book we know as the Bible. My visions of heaven are peace and happiness, friends and families reunited. Lord help us not to be worried about going to heaven as you will be there to care for us all forever.

Amen

Rebecca Holden, aged 9

Dear God

Heaven is above the clouds so far away from here. When we die we will go to heaven but only if we have been really good and we will stay longer up in heaven. We thank you for our life on earth. Help us to be really good so that we can come to heaven when we die and

know that we will be safe where nobody
does nasty things to other people like they
do on earth.

     Amen

Gail Stanley, aged 9

Heaven
    Horses, horses galloping around
    angels with halos their bright and
                  dazzling crowns,
    Jesus is the light of the world,
    he sits upon a cloud.
    Bright beaming lights shining from him,
    a purple robe as a gown.
    I wish I could find out,
    I will someday
    It will be a perfect time out.

     Amen

Laura Perry, aged 11

9

Our home and families

Dear Lord

We thank you for our warm home, that we are able to come home and know that we will be safe. Thank you that there are people in our homes that care for us. Let us remember people who don't have homes to go to.

Amen

Lisa Potts

Dear God

Be with us in our homes today
when we work and when we play.

Amen

Ashley Evans, aged 7

Dear Lord

Thank you so much for our families. Thank you so much for our grandmas and grandads. Let us remember how special they are and thank you for all the time they spend with us by taking us for walks and all the exciting stories and games they play with us.

Amen

James White, aged 10

Dear God

Please bless all the family, please let us remember people who haven't got a family. Let us try and think about how sad it would be if we had nobody around to talk to and play with.

Amen

Charlotte Ball, aged 8

Dear God

Thank you for our mummys and daddies and all our family. Thank you for little children. They are so nice to play with. Thank you for our homes that we live in.

Amen

Anju Midda, aged 7

Dear Lord

Thank you that we have a house to live in, that we have lots of furniture in our houses that we can sit on. It is sad that some people have no home or furniture. Help us to be good and kind always.

Amen

Jagjot Randhawa, aged 7

Our home and families

Dear Lord

Thank you for our families. You are the father of all the families in the world. Every family is special to you. Help us all to work together as a family.

Amen

Lisa Potts

10

Our friends

Dear God

It's so good that we can have friends to share secrets with and to play with. Jesus had many friends, as we have. Let us remember how well he treated his friends and hope that we will be able to follow you always.

Amen

Lisa Potts

Dear God

Thank you for my friends, that I can play with them and say jokes to them. Let us be really nice to them and not horrible, as friends are very special.

Amen

Clare Brown, aged 7

Dear God

Thank you for friends. Thank you God for my best friend but help us all to try very hard to be friends with everybody even if we don't like them much because I know that you love us all.

Amen

Jennifer Francis, aged 8

Dear God

I love to play with my friends. Help us to be able to be friends with the people who are lonely and have no friends. Let us not laugh or be nasty to our friends as they are all really, really special to you.

Amen

Emily Griffiths, aged 8

Dear God

Thank you for all our friends at church. Thank you that we can do all the jobs like cleaning the church and making the tea and putting the flowers into pots to make it look nice for a Sunday.

Amen

Laura Fox, aged 7

Dear God

Please let us be kind to people including our friends. Let us not bully people as we wouldn't like to be bullied. I hope that you will stop people from being horrible to others.

Amen

Anna Mair, aged 7

Dear God

It is really nice that I have lots of friends to play with at school. Let me be nice to them all every day.

Amen

Daniella Dailey, aged 5

Dear God

You want us all to live together as friends. Let's remember to be kind and share our differences with our friends. Please teach us that we should try and be friends with everybody no matter what colour, shape or size they are.

Amen

Lisa Potts

11

People at work

Dear God

Thank you for doctors and nurses that help us. Thank you for medicine and tablets that you have made so that we can get better quickly when we are poorly. Thank you for these special people.

Amen

Kirsty Spence, aged 7

Dear God

So many people in the world go out to work each day. There are so many different jobs that people do. God, let us remember that everybody has a different skill and there is no one job better than another. Let us remember those people who have no work. Please help them to find work.

Amen

Lisa Potts

Dear God

I thank you so much for doctors and nurses. They are so special as they always help sick people. They not only work in the day but at night times when we are asleep. They always think of others before themselves.

Amen

Serena Smallman, aged 9

Dear God

Please look after people who save lives, people like firemen and women who rescue people in fires as they can get burnt really easily. Please help police men and women as their job is very hard and dangerous because they have to stop people from taking drugs and stealing things.

Amen

Gemma Plant, aged 11

Dear Lord

We thank you for people who go to work and earn money to buy lovely things for us. We thank you for those who work to help other people like doctors, nurses paramedics and people who help us to get better when we are ill.

We do pray for those people who are out of work, those who have little money and find it hard to cope. We pray for them also. Dear Lord keep watch over all the people who are at work.

Amen

Charlotte Warshern, aged 10

Dear God

I pray for bus drivers and train drivers as they have a very hard job because they have to look after so many people on their buses and trains and they have to take them to so many different places around the country.

Amen

Simon Hughes, aged 9

Dear God

Thank you, Lord, that we have people in this world who work voluntarily for no money for different charities. If it wasn't for them these charities wouldn't be able to run properly.

Amen

Lisa Potts

12

Our school

Dear God

Thank you for school and for all the fun things we do at school. Thank you for our teachers who work hard so that we can learn new tasks each day.

Amen

Lisa Potts

Dear God

I like school. Thank you that I have lots of friends at school and that we can all play together when we are at school. Help us to be able to be sensible at school and kind to everyone.

Amen

Sarah Williams, aged 8

Dear Lord

I hope you are all right. Thank you for crayons, because we can colour in with them at school. Thank you for our teachers and thank you for our school. Sometimes I really like school and I love reading books with lots of pictures in.

Amen

Laura Vaughan, aged 5

Dear Lord

Thank you for school that we can learn to do good for other people, for teachers who help us to do our best so that we can go on and teach other people the work of the Lord. Let us not do bad things at school and to learn to be just like you.

Lord, thank you so much for schools.

Amen

Elizabeth Holbrook, aged 10

Dear God

Thank you for our schools. Thank you for the lollipop ladies who help us to get safely to school.

Thank you for the dinner ladies who serve food and take care of injuries.

Thank you for friends who play with us. Help us to be kind to other people when we are at school.

Amen

Andrew Bennett, aged 9

Dear Lord

Thank you for the hard work that teachers put in so that we learn how to lead a hard-working life. You made us really clever in lots of ways and this is good as it wouldn't be very good if we all did the same job. So thank you God for teachers.

Amen

Katherine Hall, aged 8

Dear God

Thank you for schools. It is sad that there are children who don't go to school like us because they have run away from home or because they live in very poor countries where there aren't many schools at all.

I hope that one day every child will go to school all over the world.

Amen

Paul Harvey, aged 9

Dear Lord

School is a very special place. Let us be thankful for our school and everything that we do in school like reading, writing and maths. Thank you for stories that we hear and the pictures that we paint, the music and games and dance that we do. Thank you, Lord, for all the schools in this country and schools all over the world.

Amen

Lisa Potts

13

Happy and sad days

Dear Lord

You are so special. We thank you for all the wonderful things you give us, for families and friendships, for fun and laughter, for all the good times we can share together. Let us never forget these special times.

Amen

Lisa Potts

Dear Jesus

You are so nice. You have made so many nice things in the world and I am happy a lot of the time.

Amen

Taishon Wynter, aged 5

Dear God

Thank you for this happy day, for all the fun we've had. Thank you for letting me have a happy time with all my friends today.

You have given me so much on this happy day and you have given this beautiful weather.

All I want to say to you Lord is THANK YOU.

Amen

Lizzie Dale, aged 9

Dear Lord

There are times when we feel sad and lonely. Let us never forget that you love me and everyone I know.

Amen

Olivia Washer, aged 5

Dear Lord

Help us to together bind,
In our thoughts and in our mind,
When times are rough,
And when times are bad,
Help us not to be down or sad,
We know you're there,
We know that you care.
Thank you dear Lord for being our
shield and sword.

Happy and sad days

When we're sad and when we cry
Our faith in you does never die,
When you're here we have no fear,
Lord in heaven above,
We will always have your love.
Thank you dear Lord, for being our
                    shield and sword.

Amen

Amy Brettel, aged 10

Dear Lord

Sometimes situations are difficult. Help
me Lord to get through tough times. At
the end of the day it's you we turn to in
work and in play. When things go wrong
we know you're there with lots of helpful
thoughts to share.

Amen

Elizabeth Crofts, aged 10

Dear Lord

Today I pray for people who will be unhappy because they have no money for food or clothes. I pray for poorly people in the world who have no money for medicine. Help them, Lord, to try and be happy.

Amen

Lisa Potts

14

Busy days

Dear Lord

Thank you Lord for busy days. They are so special when we are dashing around on our bikes with our friends having lots of fun. Thank you for all the lovely places that we can go like parks, farms, swimming. Let us be grateful for all these lovely places.

Amen

Lizzie Hartley, aged 10

Dear God

I like being at home helping my mum to cook and clean, and I like playing with my brothers and sisters with all our toys. Thank you God that I am busy.

Amen

Maryam Mir, aged 7

Dear God

I am so glad that there are times when we are really busy doing all sorts of fun things. Thank you that we can go out in the open air to play but also thank you that we can be busy indoors with books, cooking, watching television, making and creating new things. Thank you, Lord, that you give us this special time.

Amen

Lisa Potts

Dear God

I like to be busy and play with my toys. It is nice that I can have busy days.

Amen

Christal Cambell, aged 7

Dear God

Busy days, busy days,
I work hard on busy days.
Thank you for all the teachers
who help us with hard questions.
Busy days – thank you Lord for busy
                                        days.
Busy days, busy days,
oh thank you Lord for busy nights.
Thank you for all the people
who work very hard day and night.
Oh thank you Lord for busy days.

   Amen

Matthew Gurney, aged 10

Dear God

Thank you God for busy days that we
have to cope with. I hope we still have
time to think of you at the end of a day.

We thank you that we can rest and think of you and all the good work that you do.

Amen

Steven Hall, aged 10

Dear God

Thank you for busy days at home at school and everywhere we go. Please look after us and care for us always.

Amen

Oliver Dale, aged 7

Dear Father God

Let us be grateful that we can spend time learning new skills. Help us to be patient and understanding towards other people even when we are very busy.

Amen

Lisa Potts

15

Day and night

Dear Lord

Thank you for all
the days of the week
and all the months
of the year. Let us
remember that when
each day has gone it

won't be coming back, so help us to try
and do good work each day.

Amen

Lisa Potts

Dear Lord

I like day time that we can go out and play in the sunshine. It makes me very happy.

Amen

Francesca Quintyne, aged 5

Dear God

Thank you for the moon and the stars that come out at night time. We don't get to see them much as we are fast asleep in bed. Thank you God lots and lots.

Amen

Benjamin Augustus Bailey, aged 6

Day and night

Dear God

Thank you for the night and the day, for the sun and the stars and the thunder and the lightning and the clouds and the rain. Thank you for the big bright moon.

Amen

Christina Bennett, aged 7

Dear God

I really like the day time as the sunshine comes out and we can play outside, but it is also fun at night time when Mr Moon comes out to watch over us when we go to sleep. Thank you for night and day times.

Amen

Amardeep Sidhrar, aged 7

Dear Lord

When we wake up in the morning we thank you for the new day ahead of us. Help us to fill the day with lots of happiness so we can go to bed knowing that we have filled the day the way you wanted it to be.

Amen

Lisa Potts

Dear Lord

Thank you lord for the day and the night time. We can play and then we can go to sleep.

Amen

Nicholas Vaughan, aged 4

16

Ourselves

Dear Father God

Your made us all. Thank you that we are healthy. Let us think about those people who are blind and cannot see. Also people who have special needs and need extra help and people who are in wheelchairs because they cannot walk. Let us not make fun of these people and help us not to take ourselves for granted.

Amen

Lisa Potts

Dear Father God

Thank you Lord for my hands and feet, that I can climb trees and ride my bike, write and paint nice pictures.

Thank you God.

Amen

Christopher Swatman, aged 7

Dear Lord

Thank you for my eyes so that I can see all the pretty things that you made for us all to look at.

Thank you God.

Amen

Laura Fox, aged 6

Dear God

Thank you for my teeth. Let me try and keep them clean so I can eat nice food.

Amen

Marium Begum, aged 5

Dear God

Thank you for my brain because without my brain I wouldn't be able to think about nice things.

Amen

Naresh Chopra, aged 7

Dear Lord

Thank you for my hands. Without my hands I wouldn't be able to carry things or write stories or play on the computer.

Amen

Daniel Sekhon, aged 7

Dear God

Let us take care of ourselves. Help us to eat good food so we can grow strong. Let us be honest to ourselves and let us grow into good, kind adults.

Amen

Lisa Potts

17

Weather and seasons

Dear God

Thank you for the thunder and lightning. It is very scary and I'm glad it doesn't happen all the time as I would never be able to play outside.

Amen

Maariyah Pathan, aged 5

Dear God

Thank you
for rainy days,
that they feed
the plants to
make them
grow. I love
watching the
rain drops on
the window
and listening
to the lovely
sound they
make.

Amen

Leanne Wills, aged 7

Dear Jesus

It is very windy today. I love to watch the wind blowing the leaves off the trees and blowing the washing dry. Thank you Lord for windy days.

Amen

Felicity Summerfield, aged 8

Dear God

I love the summer as you can play outside and you can eat ice cream.

Amen

Helen Davis, aged 5

Dear Lord

Thank you for all the different types of weather, for the wind, rain, sun, snow, frost and cloudy days. It is so amazing that you made all of these and without each one every day would be the same.

Amen

Lisa Potts

Dear God

Thank you
for summer
and winter, for
the times when
we can play
outside in the
hot weather
and for the times when we can play in the
snow and build snowmen. Help us never
to forget that you made all the seasons.

Amen

Anna Prothero, aged 8

Dear God

You made all of the seasons; each one of them is so different. We can learn so many different things from each season, all the new animals and flowers in the spring and summer and all the trees and flowers that lose their leaves and petals in the autumn and winter.

Let us try not to take all of this for granted.

Amen

Lisa Potts

18

Animals and pets

Dear Father God

We thank you for all the animals in the world. You made every single one. All of them are so different. Help us to take care of them all.

Amen

Lisa Potts

Dear Lord

Thank you for all the animals in the world. Thank you for the pets which can stay at home with us. Thank you for wild animals for us to look at when we go into the countryside. All of these animals are so special to you Lord.

Amen

Emily Hills, aged 8

Dear Lord

Animals are killed for their skins like tigers but whales are killed for oil, and elephants for their tusks. Please Lord let people leave the animals in the world alone so they can live on and on.

Amen

Rhiannon Evans, aged 9

Dear Lord

Thank you that we are able to have pets. Let us remember that all pets are special. We thank you that you made them for us to spend time in our houses help us to treat them with great care.

Amen

Amy Probert, aged 8

Dear Lord

Thank you for all the world's animals. Please help all the animals whose homes are being destroyed by deforestation. Please help as well the animals who are being kept in captivity when they should be free. Also Lord help all those animals who are sick. We ask this in your name.

Amen

Rebecca Downs, aged 12

Dear God

Thank you for all the beautiful animals that you have made. Let us remember that they are just like people so we should be nice to them.

Amen

Christina Bennett, aged 7

Dear Lord

Let us remember those animals in the world that are becoming very rare. This is very sad as soon there will be some animals that we will never see. Please take care of them all.

Amen

Lisa Potts

19

Helping and caring

Dear God

I know that you care about each and every one of us. You made us all and we are all so special to you. We are also so different from one another. Let us learn from you to care for one another and to treat each other with respect.

Amen

Lisa Potts

Dear Lord

Help us to care for our mummys and daddies, brothers and sisters. Thank you God that I have a mummy and daddy that love me and tuck me in at bed time.

Amen

Sam Carter, aged 6

Dear Lord

Help us to care about people who are ill in hospital. There are a lot of children who have serious illnesses such as cancer and lukemia. Let us remember that they are sometimes sad. Please help them through life. Lord help clever people to work hard in finding cures to help them.

Amen

Shelly Holmes, aged 9

Dear God

Let me help all of the people who are nice forever and let me care for my friends.

Amen

April Anderson, aged 4

Dear God

Let us care about you always and let us grow like you more and more every day. You are so special and you care about everybody in this world. Help people to go to church and pray to you so they will be nice people.

Amen

Kathryn Crofts, aged 9

Dear Lord

I care about all my friends and my mummy and daddy and sisters and brother. I hope that other people care about their mummies and daddies like I do.

Amen

Francesca Bennett, aged 5

Dear Lord

Help us to forgive one another more easily. Help us to appreciate the people who care for us around us. Lord, please put love into our hearts so that we can always love you and everyone around us.

Amen

Lisa Potts

20

Our world

Dear God

You created this wonderful world that we live in. Please help us to love one another. God, help nations to be kind and friendly to other nations. Help us to try and bring peace to the world and to make the world a safer and more caring place.

      Amen

Lisa Potts

Dear God

Thank you for the world. Thank you for making the sun and moon. Thank you for making me and everyone. Thank you for making creatures. What a happy world we live in.

Thank you for making day and night. Thank you for making sea and sky.

Thank you for making grass and earth. What a happy world we live in.

Thank you for making buildings. Thank you for making churches and homes. Thank you for making every one in this world.

Amen

Rebecca D'cruze, aged 10

Dear Lord

Please help the people in the third world countries who are not as fortunate as us. We have birthday and Christmas presents but most of these people have nothing. Let us be thankful that we have so many good things in our lives.

Amen

Rebecca Holden, aged 9

Dear Lord

Thank you for all the charities in the world. Help us to give money so that people who are poor or who are ill can get better and be happy.

Amen

Zeleica Malan, aged 9

Dear Father

Help the children that don't have any food because they are poor. Please help these children especially those in Africa. Please keep them all safe.

Amen

Heather Coyle, aged 7

Dear Lord

Please be with all of the people in Rwanda, Bosnia and all of the people who are in other countries who are facing the problems of war. Please be with them and keep them safe. Give the fighters peace in their mind. They will sense eventually. Let us think about people who have no food and are very skinny.

Amen

Laura Perry, aged 11

Dear God

Please guide all the leaders of the world when they meet up and try and make the world we live in a safer place. Please take care of all the children in every country. Keep them safe from danger and help them to know that you are always with them.

Amen

Lisa Potts